ST. ANTHONY CHORALE

from

***Variations on a Theme* by Joseph Haydn**

I - 8's and 4's
II - 8's and 4's to 1
Ped. 16' to 1

Music by
JOHANNES BRAHMS
Arranged by
HERMENE WARLICK EICHHORN

18
I
p
Ped. to II off
23
28
f Box open
33

37
II p
add Ped. to II
43
f add 16'
49
54